All Stuck Together

Written by Sarah Snashall

Illustrated by Amberin Huq

Once upon a time, a mighty oak grew at the foot of a mountain. Its leaves hit the clouds and its branches sang with birds.

One day, a woodcutter found the tree.
He threw his arms around its thick trunk.

"This tree will make me rich," he laughed.

As his first blow hit the tree, a thousand birds exploded into angry tweets. With the second blow, the birds flew into the air.

With the third blow, the birds began to swirl around and around the woodcutter.

"Ouch!" he shouted as the birds drove him out of the forest.

The next day, the woodcutter sent his servant, Jack, to chop down the tree.

Jack looked up at the mighty oak.

"Few trees are as fine as this one," the boy thought out loud. "I cannot be the person who destroys it."

"The tree is home to many happy birds," called a man.

A funny little hermit was perched behind some low ferns.

"If you need wood, perhaps you could cut down this silver birch?" the hermit asked.

He pointed to a tree that sprouted near him.

Jack agreed. In a few quick blows, the silver birch was on the ground. Tucked inside the hollow tree stump was a bird as golden as the sun.

"Thank you for saving my tree," the hermit said. "This bird is a gift for you. She will lay golden eggs like this. But do not let people stroke her."

"Thank you!" Jack shouted as he ran off to sell the first egg.

When Jack got to the market, some boys and girls ran up to the golden bird.

"DON'T!" Jack shouted. But it was too late.

"Oh!" one girl cried. "Help!"

Her hand had stuck to the bird like glue.

A herb seller tried tugging at the girl's blue skirt.

"Oh!" she cried. "I'm stuck too!" And she was.

Mrs Drew the toy maker came over.

"Grab my shirt," the herb seller shouted.

But it was no good. Now Mrs Drew was stuck.

Soon, thirteen hot and thirsty people were stuck to the golden bird!

"Stop!" shouted Jack. "No new helpers, please!"

"Let's go and see the king," said Jack. "Perhaps he can help."

So, all stuck together, they set off for the royal villa.

Now, the king had a little girl called June who had never laughed. Today was her birthday.

As she looked sadly out of the window, she spotted an odd sight …

A whole line of people were stuck to a golden bird! June had never seen such a funny sight.

A joyful feeling grew in June's tummy. The corners of her mouth began to curl up. She threw open the window and … laughed out loud!

Just like that, every person stuck to the golden bird was free!

And from then on, when Jack went to the market to sell the golden eggs, he left the bird at home.

Phonics Practice

Say the sound and read the words.

long /oo/	-ew

crew   threw   brew   grew   shrew   blew

/y+oo/	ew

stew   few   dew   mildew   nephew   skewer

/ur/	ir

bird   shirt   skirt   third   first   thirteen

/ur/	er

herb   term   stern   expert   person   desert

Can you say your own sentences using some of the words on these pages?

What other words do you know that are spelled in these ways?

/ou/	ou

mountain   scout   proud   hound
round   sound

/oi/	oy

boy   toy   destroy   enjoy   royal   annoy

Common exception words

any   eyes   friends   once   please   oh

We may say some words differently because of our accent.

Talk about the story

Answer the questions:

1 Why did the woodcutter laugh when he saw the tree?

2 What warning did the hermit give to Jack about the golden bird?

3 How many people were all stuck together?

4 How did June's laugh help Jack?

5 Have you ever been stuck to something? What happened?

6 Does this story remind you of any others you've read? Can you describe them?

Can you retell the story in your own words?

AFTER READING

Try these activities with your child:

★ Imagine you are Jack. Make a birthday card for your new friend, June.

★ What do you think the king might have said about June laughing? Draw a picture of the king with June and add speech bubbles to show what they would say.

★ How many *oy* words can you find in the story? Look back through the story and count or write them down.

Reading tip

Make reading together part of your child's daily routine. Encourage your child to join in with familiar books or to share the reading of a new story with you.

ISBN: 978 1 3983 2612 5

Text, design, illustrations and layout © 2021 Hodder & Stoughton Limited

First published in 2021 by Hodder & Stoughton Limited (for its Rising Stars imprint, part of the Hodder Education Group),

An Hachette UK Company

Carmelite House, 50 Victoria Embankment, London EC4Y 0DZ

www.risingstars-uk.com

Impression number 10 9 8 7 6 5 4 3 2
Year 2025 2024 2023 2022 2021

Author: Sarah Snashall
Series Editor: Abigail Steel
Senior Publisher: Helen Parker
Development Editor: Sasha Morton
Illustrator: Amberin Huq / Plum Pudding
Academic Consultant: Professor Clare Wood
Educational Consultants: Debbie Hepplewhite and Helen Marron
Brand design: Amparo Barrera, Kneath Associates
Design concept: Mo Choy Design
Page layout: Lorraine Inglis
Editorial: Gaelle Lefevre, Jane Jackson

With thanks to the schools that took part in the development of Reading Planet, including:
Fairway Primary School, Stockport; Irthlingborough Nursery & Infant School; Mile Oak School, Brighton; Salusbury Primary School, London; St Augustine's Catholic Primary School, Coventry; and St John's Primary School, Kenilworth.

All rights reserved. Apart from any use permitted under UK copyright law, no part of this publication may be reproduced or transmitted in any form or by any means, electronic or mechanical, including photocopying and recording, or held within any information storage and retrieval system, without permission in writing from the publisher or under licence from the Copyright Licensing Agency Limited. Further details of such licences (for reprographic reproduction) may be obtained from the Copyright Licensing Agency Limited: https://www.cla.co.uk/

A catalogue record for this title is available from the British Library.

Printed in Dubai

Hachette UK's policy is to use papers that are natural, renewable and recyclable products and made from wood grown in well-managed forests and other controlled sources. The logging and manufacturing processes are expected to conform to the environmental regulations of the country of origin.

Orders: Please contact Hachette UK Distribution, Hely Hutchinson Centre, Milton Road, Didcot, Oxfordshire, OX11 7HH. Telephone: +44 (0)1235 400555. Lines are open from 9 a.m. to 5 p.m., Monday to Friday. Email: primary@hachette.co.uk

MIX
Paper from responsible sources
FSC™ C104740

Target Practice

Target phonemes/graphemes

long /oo/ **-ew** /ou/ **ou**
/y+oo/ **ew** /oi/ **oy**
/ur/ **ir er**

GREEN
Reading Planet Level 5

Phonics Phase 5

All Stuck Together

When people stroked Jack's golden bird they all got stuck together. Who can set them free?

More books in the series

Bird Boy

My Lapland Trip

The Worst Show in the World

Animals, Where Are You?

Retelling/traditional tale

www.risingstarsreadingplanet.com

ISBN 978-1-3983-2612-5

9 781398 326125

FSC